YOU NEED IT

BY JILL EGGLETON

ILLUSTRATED BY KATIE McCORMICK

TALK BOX

Get the Latest NOW!

NEW DIGIFONE – MORE FEATURES THAN EVER!

- Create your own playlists with the in-built music player and share them with your friends.
- Snap photos and videos with the integrated camera.
- Play the latest 3-D games.
- Voice identification ensures security.
- Obliterates external sounds.
- Available in six hot colours!

Want one now? Better hurry – they're flying out the door!

Freephone 0800 2276

3

NOW
a cellphone
FOR YOU!
Look!

- Dial by voice – no need to remember numbers!
- Automatic cut-off after no direct speaking.
- Automatic locator feature.
- Slim design fits in your pocket easily.

SPECIAL FEATURE:
self-focusing camera!

Slim…
Sleek…
Simple…

Salesperson will call for
free demonstration
Phone 769-834-20

QUESTION

How does the
advertisement grab
attention?

STIX

OPINION

Do you think this
advertisement would
be effective?
Why or why not?

STIX

PERSUASIVE TOOLS

rhetorical question
(does not require an answer)

simile   slang   repetition

Find any? What effect do
they have?

TARGET AUDIENCE

Who is it?

Why?

FACT OR OPINION?

What is fact?

What is opinion?

Nicole's wearin' `em . . .
Kate's wearin' `em . . .
Penny's wearin' `em . . .
Everyone's wearin' `em . . .

Phone Groovy Chicks
on 789-043-52
or visit:
www.groovychicks.

Groovy Chicks

Don't be snapped in last year's model.

You need to be wearin' `em, too . . . if you want to be with it!

Groovy Chicks

8

* Designer colours and removable frames.
* Colour-coordinate with your outfits!

QUESTION

How does the advertisement grab attention?

Hurry, they're walking out the door!

PERSUASIVE TOOLS

hyperbole (exaggeration)

imperative

metaphor

slang

Find any?

What effect do they have?

Now!

Large, lightweight hold-all.

Adjustable straps!

Phone 08-57-324
or see stock at all

Redoubt Stores

Free fold-up umbrella with every purchase. Hurry, stocks limited!

QUESTION

What is the advertiser doing to encourage the reader to buy?

Easy-access colour-coded compartments for keys, umbrella, glasses!

Amazing Feature - compartments light up. No more frantic searching!

PERSUASIVE TOOLS

hyperbole

imperative

alliteration

Find any? What effect do they have?

ALL that stuff

You can't have a bag big enough.

JUST ARRIVED
- JUMBO BAG

PERSUASIVE TOOLS

colloquialism
(informal language)

rhetorical question
hyperbole

Find any? What effect do
they have?

What are the positive benefits for the buyer?

- Deodorised
- Zip-off dirty diaper compartment
- Built-in bottle warmer and sterile unit

Do you need it? **YES!** If you have a rugrat!

Visit www.jumbo.co

B.

THE **WOW** FACTOR!

You'll have it.
Fast and made to Last

The **only** shoes worn
by champions!

Available at leading *Bromley* outlets
Visit www.bromley.co or phone 389-4

FACT OR OPINION?

The only shoes worn
by champions...

Why?

PERSUASIVE TOOLS

imperative   rhyme
          colloquialism
hyperbole

Find any? What effect do
they have?

Durable
Flexible
Waterproof
Sweat-proof

and...
spongy inner
moulded to your
foot shape

Shoo 4 You

Available online at
www.shoo4you.co

* Latest **HOT** colours!
* Funky designs for any look!
* We have just the...
* **Shoo 4 You!**

REMOVABLE DECALS FREE!

Soft and comfortable -
keep cool in summer and
warm in winter.

16

Fashionable

Flexible

CLARIFY

decals

Elegant

Sophisticated

PERSUASIVE TOOLS

slang   rhyme

colloquialism

Find any? What effect do
they have?

17

PARADISE
RETREAT
BEACH RESORT AND SPA

A piece of paradise, where often the only signs of life are the footprints of the crabs scuttling backwards and forwards on the silky white sand. Be lulled to sleep by the music of the ocean and the swaying palm trees.

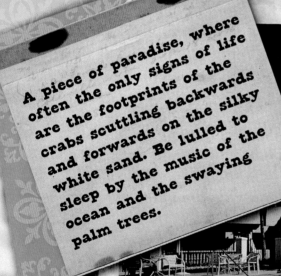

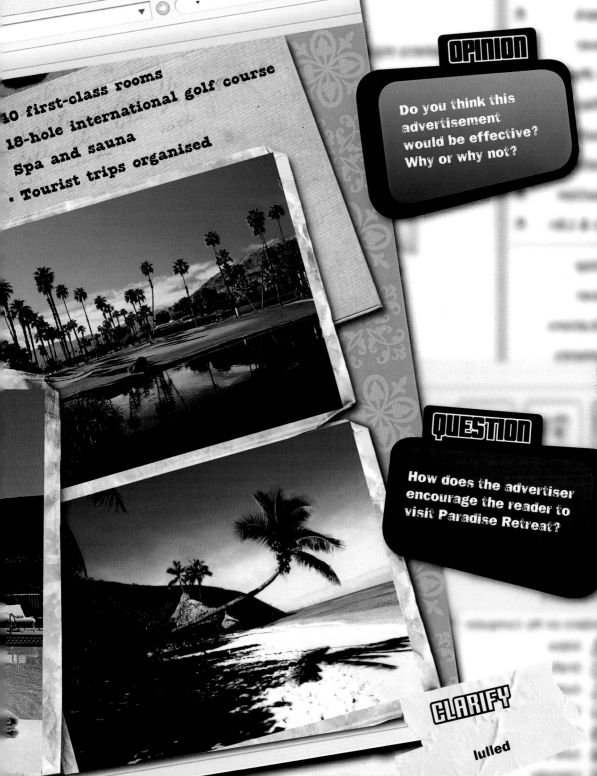

40 first-class rooms

18-hole international golf course

Spa and sauna

· Tourist trips organised

OPINION

Do you think this advertisement would be effective? Why or why not?

QUESTION

How does the advertiser encourage the reader to visit Paradise Retreat?

CLARIFY

lulled

MAGGIE'S
Affordable Holidays

FACT OR OPINION?

What is fact?
What is opinion?

QUESTION

How does the advertiser
personalise the
advertisement? What
effect does this have?

POPPIES

Going on holiday has never been so easy.

Large, fully-fenced grounds
Daily organised entertainment

Available for hire: bikes, trikes, scooters, pedal cars

FOOD FIT FOR KINGS... AND KIDS!

Let the people at POPPIES take care of YOU.

Ask about babysitters and adjoining family rooms. Visit www.poppies.co

FREEGO

Have you heard?

If you haven't heard, then you
haven't read FREEGO magazine.

People in the know read . . .
FREEGO!

www.freego.co

FREEG

FR

24

INFORM
ENTERTAIN
ENLIGHTEN

Available from all booksellers and supermarkets.

FREEGO

FR

ILLBILLY

Top 10 spot
to vis

The Great
Band E

VENTURE

THE ULTIMATE MAG FOR THE ULTIMATE ADVENTURER

A QUICK FLICK AND YOU'LL FIND **IRRESISTIBLE** READING

SUBSCRIBE NOW AND **WIN** AN AWESOME **TRAVEL PRIZE** PLUS $1000 WORTH OF EQUIPMENT AND CLOTHING!

ENDORSED BY THE OUTDOOR ADVENTURE CLUB

YES! Of course I want to subscribe.
ONLY $36 for six issues.

Name ---------------------------------

Address----------------------------------

Phone----------------------------------

Email ----------------------------------

Cheque/
Credit Card ☐☐☐☐☐☐☐

Signature ----------------------------

THINK ABOUT THE TEXT

What connections can you make to advertisements and the effect they have on you?.

wanting something
you can't afford

becoming annoyed with
message bombardment

making an
unconsidered
decision to buy

TEXT TO SELF

avoiding
manipulation

facing the challenge
of distinguishing
between fact and
exaggeration

wanting something
because other people
have it

wanting
something
you don't
need

TEXT TO TEXT

Talk about other texts you may have
read that have similar features.

TEXT TO WORLD

Talk about situations in the world that
might connect to elements in the text.

PLANNING AN ADVERTISEMENT

1. Choose a product or service to advertise.

2. Think about the purpose of the advertisement.

- To inform and excite interest in the product or service.
- To influence the behaviour and attitudes of people.
- To invite further enquiries about the product or service.
- To give contact advice.

3. Think about the audience the advertisement is targeting.

- Teenagers
- Old people
- Sportspeople
- Parents.

4. Think about the way you can use language to persuade the reader. You can use . . .

- Emotive language to excite the feelings of the reader.
- Instructions that involve the reader personally.
- Rhetorical questions and hyperbole.
- Personal pronouns to involve the reader.
- Slang or colloquial language that your target audience might use.
- Text that urges action.

5. Think about the way you can use images and design to gain the attention of the reader. You can use . . .

- Striking visuals.
- Symbols or logos.
- A design that would appeal to your target audience.
- Colours that give messages.

WRITING AN ADVERTISEMENT

Have you . . .

- used words in an imaginative way – similes, metaphors, alliteration?

- used attention-grabbing headlines and captions?

- used humour?

- used promises or special offers aimed at the reader?

- used rhetorical questions or hyperbole?

- used slang or colloquial language?

- included images and a design that will appeal to your target audience?

Don't forget to revisit your work. Do you need to change, add or delete anything to improve your advertisement?